M. P. Gladstonian

The Great Betrayal

The invasion of East Anglia. Third Edition

M. P. Gladstonian

The Great Betrayal
The invasion of East Anglia. Third Edition

ISBN/EAN: 9783337284855

Printed in Europe, USA, Canada, Australia, Japan

Cover: Foto ©Andreas Hilbeck / pixelio.de

More available books at **www.hansebooks.com**

"East Anglia is the most vulnerable part of the country it is the part which was threatened in the days of the Great Napoleon."—*Vide* Debate in Committee of Supply, House of Commons, March 17th, 1893.

THE

Great Betrayal:

OR,

THE INVASION

OF EAST ANGLIA.

THIRD EDITION.

PRICE SIXPENCE.

THIRD EDITION.

"THE GREAT BETRAYAL."

———◆———

The EAST ANGLIAN DAILY TIMES *says:* "*Bright and most attractive . . The story is capitally told. The element of personal adventure is artistically introduced, and, leaving the ultra-Toryism out of account, the writer is to be warmly congratulated upon the rigour and 'Vraisemblance' which have rendered his work so deservedly successful.*"

DEDICATED

to

LORD RANDOLPH CHURCHILL, M.P.,

By Special Permission.

This little Sketch, which was made the subject of a leading article in THE GLOBE *of March 24th, has succeeded far beyond the Author's anticipations. It was designed, like the illustration in a novel, with the idea of interesting people who have been bored with argument; and, if it directs to the dangers of Home Rule the attention of a section of the electorate who from sheer weariness are almost persuaded to let matters take their course, the Writer's aim will have been achieved.*

THE GREAT BETRAYAL:

The Retrospect

Of a Gladstonian M.P.

HERTFORD :

PUBLISHED BY THE "HERTS. GUARDIAN" NEWSPAPER CO. (LTD.)

PREFACE.

SLIGHTLY modifying the proverb, "*Si non e vero ben trovato*," it may be said of this little sketch that, if not true, it is likely to become so. Given a certain set of causes, corresponding effects may be fairly anticipated; and upon such a basis the present writer, in 1884, ventured to foretell precisely the course Mr. GLADSTONE would take in Egypt, and the disaster that would ensue. The late Lord IDDESLEIGH, writing to the author, then expressed the fear that his predictions would prove "an owre true tale;" and they were fulfilled almost to the letter. In this instance no one desires more earnestly than the augur that events may falsify his prophecy.

The slender defences of our Eastern seaboard—an item not omitted from the calculations of Continental strategists—render not inappropriate the selection of East Anglia as a theatre of war.

With regard to the strange tragedy that closes the Spy's career, such an incident has actually occurred on active service.

"The Great Betrayal."

A Retrospect.

It is January, 1901, and I am writing this in the only safe
Asylum for the English race—Australasia.

My name is Cicero Demosthenes Jones, and I am messenger
and odd man in the office of the *Auckland Annotator*. Yes,
that is where my undoubted talents as an orator and a devo-
tee of the Jumping Cat Cult have landed me. I am known
amongst my familiars—and everyone is familiar, not to say
contemptuous, towards me—by the *soubriquet* of "Jones, M.P.;"
because I once held the position of legislator in the Parliament of the defunct British Empire. Whenever Young
Australia—represented so far as I am immediately concerned
by the *Annotator* office-boy and juniors—feels particularly
cock-a-whoop, it says, "Jones, you obsolete Gladstonian gas-
engine, just work off that last speech you made at Westmin-
ster on 'Trust the Irish Parliament.' Let's hear how Iscariot
and the rest of you managed that great Confidence Trick—

and hurry up on the rostrum as if you had a Cossack after you!"

Then I have to repeat it all *verbatim*; for they check me by an old copy of the *Daily News*, and if I omit anything, they jog my memory with the office furniture, and jeopardise my position on the rickety wooden stool. A proud elevation for a once prominent politician to occupy in the Dawn of the Twentieth Century! But I am not alone in my abnegation. There are others of my despised fraternity scattered broadcast over the great Southern Continent; and of no more account in it than a Chinaman who had pawned his pigtail would be at an Imperial audience. The thought that harasses my soul—though my associates here allege I never owned a soul that a prudent speculator would risk a brass farthing upon to redeem from Purgatory—is "How are the mighty fallen!"

The Laodicean philosopher who was Chief Secretary in Mr. Gladstone's administration is now a book-canvasser, soliciting orders for Naoroji's Decline and Fall of the Feringhee Empire; Blundella is travelling in patent medicines and quack specifics generally; the ex-chief of the Home Office is Secretary to the New Zealand Branch of the Property Nationalization Society; and the whilom Minister for War has scuttled off to herd pigs somewhere along the Pacific Slope.

These were the honest members of the Cabinet; others, more astute, are in easier circumstances, drawing their snug little annuities from St. Petersburg.

I have been asked by the enterprising proprietors of the

Annotator to record my own experiences of the catastrophe that Naoroji has so brilliantly described; and as they have promised to get me into an almshouse when my work is satisfactorily completed, I am naturally eager to begin. And yet, scorned and outlawed as I am by the worthier part of humanity, I have not sunk so low as to approach my task without shame and sorrow. Shame, at the part I and others like me played in what one who warned us vainly called " The Great Betrayal ;" and sorrow, that the halcyon days of Merrie England are gone for ever.

All the world knows how the sinister prophecy that the freest country in the world would be ruined by the son of a slaveholder was fulfilled. Heaven knows we had no lack of warning ; the brightest intellects, the most renowned statesmen and historians, the wealth, the intelligence, the experience of the nation, all pointed out a course opposite to that which we pursued ; but our Oracle had pronounced for Home Rule ; and—*quem Deus vult perdere prius dementat.*

The trouble in the East broke out six months after the establishment of the Irish Parliament ; for the lynx eyes of Gaul and Muscovite had watched us eagerly, knowing well that half a loaf would never satisfy the disciples of Healy and Parnell. Then Ireland refused supplies, scoffed at the Imperial veto, and finally declared her independence amid a tumult of acclaim from all the Parisian journals.

When it came to actual invasion, we were struck on two

sides simultaneously, and at points where we were least pre-
pared. On the South Coast, where we had been accumulating
men and material, a feint indeed was made by the enemy;
but his real attack was delivered on the north-west, with
Ireland as a *point d'appui*—and on the eastern coast, which was
practically defenceless. The assault from Ireland paralysed the
great Lancashire towns, whilst an overwhelming force, landing
in north-east Essex, executed a skilful *détour* and marched on
London.

THE SHADOW OF THE SWORD.

I well remember the day when we first realised the peril
of invasion. It was the Queen's Birthday, and at the head-
quarters of the eastern military district all was bustle and
animation. The hilly town of Camulodunum was one of the
oldest military stations in England, and on its bleak heights
had stood sentinel over the eastern marshes since the days
when York was the capital of the realm, and when Britain
itself was but a barbaric appanage of the Cæsars' Colonial
Empire.

The ground whereon the troops were reviewed that morning had quivered to the tread of many a Roman legion; the
turrets rising at intervals amidst the charming woodland
setting, still bore the scars left by Puritan round-shot in the
days of the Revolution; and the low-roofed bungalows of

the camp, though built only at the time of the Crimea, had sheltered soldiery as invincible as any that followed Roman eagle, or drove Prince Rupert's squadrons from the field.

The sun shone brilliantly, and a fresh breeze from the North Sea ruffled the black plumes of the cavalry and fluttered the standards of the line regiments, as the troops, with bands playing merrily, converged upon the review ground. The morning was altogether glorious, with just a suspicion of balminess in the air that seemed delightful after former experiences of May days black enough for the Newgate calendar, and winds that might with propriety have accompanied Dante and Virgil across the circle of ice that was one of the torments of perdition. Sullen Spring was fairly vanquished by Summer, and from country halls, sequestered farm houses, and quiet rectories in East Anglia, came stalwart squires and sturdy yeomen, and prim sedate clergymen with radiant bevies of pretty daughters—all thronging by road or rail into the old-world town, and establishing themselves in carriages, cabs, and waggons, as close as possible to the saluting point. And though reviews had been as plentiful in that ilk as salmon in a Scottish river, or as deities in the heathen mythology, even the townspeople themselves would not miss the spectacle. Alas, in a few short weeks

> "That noble army that so stirred our pride—
> So stout, so well-equipped, so trim-arrayed,
> Melted like snow-wreaths on a warm hill-side,
> And there was none to aid!"

The alignment, I remember, extended direct from north to south of that big *Campus Martius*, and faced the saluting point, which was filled with ladies in dainty summer attire. In one of these latter I was personally interested—my niece Winifred Kennedy, who was chatting gaily with a young officer of the Royal Engineers. This annoyed me at the time,. because I was anxious to have a quiet word with her regarding my friend O'Regan, M.P., who had returned from the United States in order to represent an Irish constituency.

The troops were strong upon the field that day. With the line battalions of the territorial regiments were brigaded all available auxiliaries ; for the Militia had been embodied, and the Volunteers of the Eastern District had been called out. On the right of the line were four magnificent squadrons of Dragoons, each trooper as statuesque as a Life Guard in his archway at Whitehall. Next ranked four Lancer squadrons, and these, though looking really handsome and warlike as they formed in brilliant array across the crisp turf, were in regard to numbers a mere skeleton. This unhappily, proved to be the state of all our cavalry, for the army reserve system broke down deplorably, and it was found that whilst many reserve men had disappeared altogether, numbers of others had re-enlisted surreptitiously, and had in fact been still in the Army, whilst the country supposed them available as reserves.

Next in order to the cavalry stood the Infantry Brigade, looking in the distance like a broad band of scarlet, topped with flashing steel, and relieved by a central belt of white that shone like enamel. In rear of the regulars were ranged the Militia and Volunteer battalions, and on the extreme right of the line were the spick-and-span batteries of Royal Artillery, and the hooded waggons of the Army Service Corps—the latter irreverently known as the "Mud-Tumblers." Twenty-one guns and three fusillades, with a few bars of the National Anthem given between the volleys, completed the Royal Salute, and as its last note sounded, the Commander-in-Chief—who was to present new colours to one of the crack north-country regiments—rode on the ground with a brilliant staff. The Duke having inspected the soldiery, the ceremony of trooping the old colours commenced. The band of the "Marlborough's Own" marched from right to left of the line, playing the "troop farewell." Wheeling as they faced the colours, which were stationed with their guard at the left front of the line, the band returned, playing a beautiful air from "Andreas Hofer." They then again advanced, and followed by the right, or pioneer company, once more saluted the colours, which were borne after them, as, dividing into sections, they marched slowly on either side of the long line of redcoats. After a last parade from right front to left rear of the line, the band meanwhile playing "Auld Lang Syne," the brave old colours, with their weight of emblazoned battle-honours—from "Ramilies" to "Peninsula," and from "Crimea" to "Soudan"—were furled. The senior subalterns and the colour guard having been called to the front, the new Queen's colour and regimental colour were placed across a tripod, and a martial hymn was sung by many thousand voices.

Then the Chaplain-General, in a clear, strong voice, spoke the grand majestic words of a prayer such as Cromwell might have uttered before Dunbar, or Havelock before the gates of Lucknow. Essentially a soldier's prayer, it rose in cadence anon lofty, anon supplicating. It asked that the gracious favour of the Most High might rest on those who should follow the standards then committed to their trust; that He might give them courage, resting on their confidence in Him: that they might have grace to use victory with moderation; and if it should be His will that success should not always attend them, might they yet be spared dishonour. There were many other touching sentences in this beautiful prayer at the consecration of the standards—on the eve of battle, as it proved—and I remember wondering whether we, as a nation, having abandoned the Protestants of Ireland to the fury of their hereditary foes, had merited the Divine favour that we asked. For I can recognise now the terrible guilt of that betrayal. When Irish faction no longer felt the restraining hand of England, a bitter religious war blazed out. The Ireland of Wolf Tone, of O'Connell, and McCarthy—the priest-ridden Ireland—flew at the throat of the "English garrison," and scenes that in their furious carnage resembled those of the first French Revolution were enacted. The Northern Irish were quelled after a desperate resistance; and so savage and merciless was the vengeance of the South, that even our *laisser-faire* Ministry were roused at length, and were on the point of adventuring the re-conquest of Ireland, when, on the Afghan borderland, the Muscovites broke our slender line of defence, and we lost "the brightest jewel in the British crown."

Writing, as I do, when the sun of England is set for ever; when there are "none so poor as do her reverence"—and when, too, my own faith in the Gladstonian fetish has undergone the test of experience—I have little to urge in extenuation of the blind guides who led their country into a Marah of bitterness and a Dead Sea of regrets; yet I will say that our Tory opponents lost heart too soon. Had they shown better discipline they might have retrieved their first defeat at the polls. Some of them, too, might with advantage have thought a little less of the "Grand National" and a little more of Imperial interests : whilst if they had brought themselves more into line with the democratic spirit of the age, and, sinking their own internal jealousies, had presented a level front to the forces of disintegration, they might have saved England in spite of itself.

But I will no longer dwell upon the broad outlines of what is now ancient history; let me return to the plain record of what I witnessed personally.

It was a brave ceremony, that last colour presentation. The old Duke, stout, rubicund, choleric, yet ever worthily known as the soldiers' friend, lifted the bright embroidered colours and presented them to two young lieutenants, who received them kneeling. Then H.R.H. addressed the "Marl-borough's Own" in a stirring, soldierly speech, expressing his confidence that the colours would be followed through all danger, and that every regiment of the Crown would vie with its fellow in carrying their country's standards to victory.

Just then I caught sight of O'Regan amongst the crowd at the saluting base. He was talking with a Roman Catholic priest, and the faces of both wore an earnest yet scoffing expression that struck me afterwards as peculiar. But O'Regan was always remarkable. He had risen by sheer ability from a lowly station. In his youth, as he told me, he had served in the ranks of a crack Irish regiment, which he left quite unexpectedly. He was not attractive, yet his appearance was of the kind one never forgets. His heavy watchful eyes were deep-set in a flat Tartar face that promised little intelligence : yet there seemed nothing he did not understand. He won "silk" unaided, and when he settled in a garrison town his popularity amongst the troops was immense ; for in his capacity of barrister he was at the service of the prisoner at any court-martial. By our own people—*i.e.*, the Gladstonians —he was especially admired, and in the earlier days of our last Parliament he was the familiar of the Minister for War.

O'Regan and the priest sauntered up easily to the carriage in which I sat with Winifred Kennedy ; and I was surprised to hear my parliamentary colleague commence a running fire of scathing comment upon the appearance of the soldiery. I knew that what he said was true; yet in those days we were so accustomed to take as gospel the optimist criticism of the press, that the plain facts were unpalatable. Moreover, O'Regan himself had hitherto maintained against all comers the Gladstonian opinion that we had the best of all possible armies.

He had suddenly become brutally frank. "You have been so devoted to trade and manufacture," he said, "that the only soldierly infantry on the ground is that Ireland sends you. Barring those Irish and that north-country corps, there is not a battalion here fit to take the field."

"But Waterloo was won with young soldiers—there is nothing like your young soldier for dash," I pleaded, clinging desperately to Lord Wolseley's dictum.

"Young soldiers!—that is why Waterloo was nearly lost," replied O'Regan contemptuously. "Besides, those Waterloo lads were of hardier fibre. Were the Peninsula battles won by young soldiers, or Nelson's victories by raw seamen; were Havelock's and Campbell's columns filled with boys; and what did Frederick Roberts say when he marched from Cabul to Candahar?"

"Then you believe with all the Colonels that our Army has deteriorated through Short Service?"

"Deteriorated—it is ruined! If it went into action against European soldiers to-morrow" the priest and O'Regan exchanged glances—"it would be a short shrift for every heretic amongst you."

"Really, O'Regan, you're most unpleasant."

"I'm going to tell you the truth, when it's too late," he answered. "Your regiments now have no backbone; you have sent adrift the old stamp of non-commissioned officers—men who retrieved by valour what your officers lost by stupidity; and now, though officers have improved, the lower ranks are unreliable. You found that out in South Africa, I imagine, and you are going to have it still more forcibly impressed upon you."

"O'Regan, you croak like the wizard to Lochiel."

"And with greater reason. In his case the clans were more united."

"You are rather rough upon our union of hearts. But if you talk of recent actions, surely the Desert Column proved that Englishmen are still as heroic as those who fought at Agincourt."

"I am bored by that Desert Column," replied O'Regan "It fought gallantly, I admit; but it was the pick of the Army, formed of fire-eaters from every corps. It was like the head of a spear, the rest being merely the haft."

A burst of martial music stopped him. The troops were marching past. First came the cavalry, led by the stalwart Dragoon regiment, whose troopers would have delighted the soul of Claverhouse. Their squadrons came past the saluting point in superb array, the standard borne in front by a single horseman. Their brilliant mounted band was headed by a drummer whose grey charger stept in perfect

unison with every note, as its rider deftly beat two glittering
cup-shaped drums, that might have served as drinking beakers
for the old Norse giant Thor. The lithe and sinewy Lancers
were equally successful as a spectacle. Their tossing crimson
plumes, white gauntlets, scarlet-and-blue tunics, relieved with
amber facings, formed a beautiful combination of moving
colour, whose effect was enhanced by the gleam of lance-
spears and the fluttering of bright pennants overhead. But
though they were ostensibly on a war-footing, their numbers
were slender enough to make a saint—at anyrate a military
saint—swear like a trooper.

Headed by sturdy pioneers and active signallers, came the
massed bands of the Infantry Brigade, brilliant with scarlet
and burnished brass; their drums inscribed with many battle
honours; their big drummers, adorned with tiger skins,
flourishing their gauntleted wrists aloft at intervals, and twirl-
ing their sticks in air. It was when the infantry went past
that the justness of O'Regan's criticism became apparent. The
men were undersized and immature—one could have seized
fistfuls of red cloth where there ought to have been chest
development. Many of the sergeants looked scarcely out of
their teens, and it was evident that the sturdy type of non-
commissioned officer of Crimean days had been improved out of
existence.

Conspicuous in the quaint red coat and peaked cap of an
almost extinct order, an old Chelsea pensioner stood keenly
watching the march past, and the veteran, on whose breast

glittered a wealth of medals won in some of the sternest fights of the British Army, shook his head as the infantry went by, and grumbled out: "Stole away, stole away. There's no regiments now. What discipline can there be when the company's front curves like a scimetar! I wouldn't trust colours to none of 'em"—and the severe old critic hobbled off the field.

The last of the line regiments had cleared the saluting base, and the auxiliaries were advancing in grand divisions, when the distant sound of cannonading was heard. The civilians listened phlegmatically, for from that lofty review ground we could often hear the big guns of Shoeburyness— but there was a sudden flutter amongst the brilliant group of officers forming the Duke's Staff, and the young captain of Engineers who had been chatting to Winifred, exclaimed, "By Heaven, those are not Shoebury guns! This is no place for me. *The wind sets from Landguard!*"

It was a fitting commentary on our Intelligence Department that the enemy's cannon was the first herald of their attack.

The hard turf flying from his charger's heels, a mounted orderly dashed out of the clump of lime trees that shaded the Brigade Office, and galloped to the Staff. A brief colloquy was held, and immediately afterwards the commanding officers were called to the front, and some message, clearly of weighty import, was delivered. Then each Colonel returned to his regiment. At a signal, a mighty cheer broke forth, and the

" Marlborough's Own " lifted their bearskins aloft on point of bayonet. But on the left of the line the sound was faint and fitful. The Nationalist literature with which every barrack-room was inundated, and the Nationalist propaganda that we, alas, had ourselves fostered—these had borne bitter fruit, and on the eve of active service *the Irish regiments refused to cheer for the Queen.*

" Hallo, Fitz-William—we're limbering up ! " shouted a cheery voice to Winifred's Captain of Engineers; and looking to our right we saw a group of officers hastily settling them-selves on the seats of a natty four-in-hand, which was the glory of Landguard and the pride of Harwich redoubt ; being the joint property of the officers who dwelt in those harbour fortifications. "Come early and bring your friends "—added Fitz-William's comrade, " We shall make Harwich in three half hours, and if the enemy's in the offing, we'll have a little ' At Home ! ' "

Had I reflected for a moment, I should never have enter-tained the offer so cordially made to our little party; for in regard to horsey people, " *Timeo Danaos et dona ferentes;* " but in the excitement of the moment I accepted, and we were soon whirling amid a cloud of dust towards Harwich harbour —twenty-three miles of awkward road. I shall never forget the excitement of that ride ; the officers were in the wildest of high spirits, and they clearly exulted not only in the pros-pect of immediate hostilities, but in the apprehension I was unable to conceal, as with horses at full gallop, the coach swayed and rocked to an extent that compelled Captain Fitz-William to steady Winifred with his arm. At Harwich we found great stir and excitement; the cannonading, they told us, was far seawards, and they believed the enemy must have been beaten off by a section of the fleet that was known to be patrolling the North Sea. We crossed the estuary to Landguard—which lay on the edge of a spur of sandhills opposite Harwich—and as we walked towards my villa at Felixstowe, Captain Fitz-William very bluntly and earnestly asked my consent to his union with Winifred. I had other views for my beautiful niece; but I would not run counter to her inclinations, and as she very ably seconded her lover's plea, the resolution was carried *nem.-con.*

A masterful undaunted fellow was this Fitz-William, and with his rugged eloquence he bore down all my scruples—although the Captain was an Ulster Presbyterian, my niece a Catholic, and myself—well, I believe my religion was Opportunist Nonconformity. He wrung my hand with a grip of iron, and with kindling eyes and glowing cheek, he told us of his hope and confidence in the future.

"I am not a brilliant man"—he said—"I should never take a double first at Oxford, if I coached for centuries. But with this war my chance has come—the chance of rendering some little service to the dear England that has done so much for us : of fighting for it ; making a name, for Winnie's sake ; or, if so much honour may be given me, of dying for the *alma mater* that is so near my heart. I was never Cosmopolitan, you know "—he added with a touch of irony, "and although you have made us foreigners, I claim kinship at least with the country of Shakspeare, of Nelson, and of Gordon. I think the 'English Garrison' has so borne its part in history, that 'whatever record leap to light, we never shall be shamed.'"

He spoke proudly, this young soldier; but it was the pride of race, and not of the individual; and as he spoke, Winifred's dark blue eyes flashed approval of her lover's lofty spirit, and I felt that the barrier of religion was broken down.

But Winifred, though impressionable, seldom dwelt long in the same mood. "He's rather boyish—and very North Irish, don't you think?" she said, when the Captain had returned to the low-browed fort, happy in the consciousness of love returned.

THE ASSAULT BY SEA.

The next morning passed quietly; but towards noon two brown-sailed fishing smacks came scudding in with tidings of a disaster to our fleet. There had been a great naval battle, and luck and the torpedo being—under the changed conditions of modern warfare—more potent factors than seamanship, we could only mourn the loss of so many gallant Englishmen, who, though beaten, had not been disgraced. The remnant of our fleet, we heard, was drifting disabled towards the coast of Holland; and the enemy, severely handled, had hauled off to refit. Along the shore, the Coastguard were on the alert; the Moncrieffe guns and other defences of the harbour were tested, the buoys and lightships were removed, and an attempt was made to render the old Martello Towers serviceable as rallying points by protecting them on the sea-ward front with earth-works. Strong contingents of Artillery Militia and Volunteers from Suffolk, Essex, and Norfolk, poured into Harwich and Felixstowe, and were got under canvas with all despatch. The towers, designated by various letters of the alphabet, were defended by small *smooth-bore* guns !

About nine in the evening, the enemy's ironclads were sighted, advancing steadily with all top-hamper lowered, and in fighting trim. As they drew nearer, it was seen that in rear of the battle-ships was a flotilla of small steamers, of light draught and peculiar construction, and with their decks crowded.

The artillery duel quickly opened; and as the great shot hurtled forth from Landguard Fort and the circular redoubt on the Essex side of the estuary, the windows of Harwich Church and of the trim villas crowning the cliffs at Felix-stowe were shattered by the concussion. Ever and anon the Moncrieffe guns rose as if by magic from various unsuspected quarters, and discharged their missiles at the foe, who either by accident or design dropped several shells into the town of

Harwich, which was soon on fire in several places. However, the Volunteers and a big company of railway men and dockers from the Great Eastern Company's wharves at Parkeston, did yeoman's service in extinguishing the flames. At 9.30 the enemy's leading battleship was hulled by a well-directed shot from Landguard, and blew up. Fragments of her huge guns and equipment fell on some of the troop-launches, and sunk them with all on board. The quick-firing guns of the Essex Artillery were soon after brought into action, and played great havoc with the flotilla of troops. At length, four of the enemys' ironclads, dropping anchor, steadily shelled the circular redoubt and the fort at Landguard; but the remainder of their fleet pressed forward, and steamed towards Harwich Harbour under a cross fire from the whole of the batteries.

The scene, as the enemy's war-ships approached the entrance to Harwich Harbour, will never fade from my memory. Viewed from where I stood on the cliff opposite Harwich, the whole coast line curved like a horse-shoe from the natural break-water formed by Walton-on-the-Naze to the sand-bars at the mouth of the Deben, the lower reaches of the Orwell being concealed by a screen of foliage that swayed tremulously in the rays of a young moon. Within the rim of the horse-shoe was the wedge-shaped promontory known as Landguard Point, at whose seaward extremity the frowning bastions rose over the white tents of the auxiliaries. From the fort the clear silvery beams of the electric light extended in a broadening and wavering vista, now resting on the sharp prows of the advancing battleships, and now disclosing the swift movements of the torpedo-boats. Every link in the chain of forts defending the harbour was indicated in fragmentary outline, for at the discharge of each gun a fiery cloud hovered above it in the air until driven seawards by the fitful breeze. The scene was Titanic ; the crash of the enemy's huge projectiles against fort and boulder, the whirr of the huge splinters of stone and iron shattered by mighty impact, and the rattle of the small-arms as our infantry and the enemy's marines exchanged volleys, made the din simply appalling. Few cries for aid—though for many all aid was hopeless—could be heard amid that Inferno of sound. But whilst with his leading Division the enemy essayed the passage of the estuary, he detached his entire flotilla of light draught steamers, protected by the fire of two powerful war-ships, to attempt a landing in Mill Bay, which, recessed behind the town of Harwich, was equally sheltered from the fire of Landguard and the Redoubt. But he reckoned without his host. Steady behind the low parapets of their shelter-trenches knelt the thin line of the old Fighting Fusiliers—the "Marlborough's Own." Unsupported by artillery, and deci-mated by the deadly rain of bullets from the enemy's machine guns, they sent volley after volley into the advancing flotilla, and ere the invaders could form up on the beach, the Fusiliers, with a wild shout, charged them with the bayonet. Miners and ironworkers from the North, most of them had "'listed" from sheer love of hard knocks, and driven by their athletic arms, the "Queen of Weapons"—as the British soldier once loved to call the bayonet—proved irresistible. The flotilla was repulsed, and not one-third of those who had landed escaped to tell the tale.

Suddenly the sky was lit with a lurid glow ; a tall column of white vapour rose above the fort, and a terrific detonation shook the shore.

"There goes the last of Landguard!" I thought ; and shuddered involuntarily.

But as the smoke cleared, a loud English cheer rent the air. The flagship of the enemy's fleet, in crossing the mine-field that was mysteriously connected with the penetralia of Landguard Fort, had struck a torpedo, and amid one vast sheet of flame, that crimsoned even the far horizon, eight hundred fighting men passed to their account. The shock of the explosion was felt for leagues, and the displacement of many thousand tons of water had a disastrous effect on the invaders' torpedo boats, many of which were hurled against the sides of the battleships and destroyed. Amid a perfect *feu d'enfer* the enemy crept out of the channel, and abandoned the attack ; sending, however, a few Parthian shots vengefully into the towns on either side the estuary. And now the doctors and the ambulances came into requisition ; but I will draw a veil over the horrors of that lurid night. I remember though, that in spite of all the suffering, there was great enthusiasm among the soldiery, and the Norfolk volunteers serenaded the "Marlborough's Own" with "Rule Britannia," an air which Nelson's especial countryfolk considered their exclusive property.

When I returned to my little sea-side villa I found two rooms already requisitioned for hospital purposes. But still greater was my surprise when, in the hall, I encountered O'Regan's sacerdotal friend. Winifred, I noticed, seemed silent and *distrait*; but this I attributed to the nerve tension of the last few hours.

Early next day came Captain Fitz-William, with his arm in a sling, but looking radiant. He did not tell us that his signal gallantry had been referred to in orders that morning; this I learnt later.

Winifred became amiable with an effort, and with the Captain visited some of the wounded, who brightened up wonderfully in his cheery presence.

There was serious news afloat, however. Though foiled in their attack on Harwich, which they had designed to seize as a *depôt* for supplies and as a landing place for troops on the march to London, the enemy had effected a landing in north-west Lancashire, finding revolted Ireland a convenient base. Several sea-coast towns had been shelled, and the enemy had brutally disregarded the ordinary usages of war. On the North Sea littoral, too, Yarmouth and Lowestoft had suffered terribly.

A DELUSIVE CALM.

Meanwhile the whole country thrilled at the tidings of East Anglia's gallant and successful defence. The *Te Deum* was chanted in our disestablished churches ; and the psalm that tells how the proud were robbed and the meek were helped, was appointed to be read in chapels. Nonconformists had indeed especial cause for gratitude at the enemy's repulse, since their votes had been mainly cast for the measure that betrayed their Ulster brethren to the Irish Clerical party, and brought on all our troubles.

The Government now recovered tone somewhat, and its official organ—the *Daily Apologiser*—which, when Ireland was first occupied by the enemy, had recommended the payment of a huge indemnity, the cession of Gibraltar, the Isle of Wight, and the Channel Isles, and the neutralisation of the port of Liverpool, now valiantly declared that not even five acres and a cow should be surrendered. A determined effort was made to raise supplies ; for the Exchequer had been drained by hasty, yet ineffective, war expenditure ; and we had no revenues from Scotland or Wales, those countries having proclaimed neutrality, on the ground that they were separate states, and that the war was none of their choosing. However, by suspending the salaries and allowances of members of Parliament, the Chancellor of the Exchequer realised

a considerable sum, and as the class of adventurers returned
to the Very Last Parliament of Queen Victoria lived chiefly
by peculation, they scarcely felt the loss of their fixed
incomes.

O'Regan, I remember, was particularly well-financed about
this period.   I saw nothing of him during the assault upon
the harbour defences; but after the repulse he was a constant
visitor, and a highly entertaining companion.   He was most
courteous to Winnie, and clearly anxious to relieve the loneli-
ness she felt as a result of her lover's earnest attention to
duty.   Thus ten days passed uneventfully, until one evening,
on my return from London—for I had sustained heavy losses
in regard to my Lancashire property, and there was much to
arrange—I was shocked by the news that Winnie had met
with an accident whilst driving, and was dangerously ill.
O'Regan, who said the mishap was indirectly due to his
thoughtlessness, had already obtained surgical aid, and urged
me not to risk a conflict of medicos by calling in our own
physician.   Next morning, as I was nervously pacing the
lawn, I was called into the house by the announcement that
a Corporal of Royal Engineers wished to speak with me.

In the library I found a bronzed, square-set fellow, whose
aquiline nose, firm jaw, and steadfast eye bespoke the born
soldier.   He saluted, and after standing for a moment at
attention, said: "Could I be havin' half a word wid ye,
Sor?"   "Certainly," I answered; but the visitor seemed ill at
ease, and still he stood at "Attention."   He twirled his cap

awkwardly, and at length he continued : " Me name's Corporal McNeil, an' I've come to see ye, sor, about the bhoy."

" Boy," I answered, " What boy ? "

"Savin' your presence, it's Captain Fitz-William. I'm his servant, sor—and yours."

Then I remembered having noticed this man about the Captain's quarters.

" Ye see, sor," he continued, " I've known the Captain a power of years, and take an interest in 'um. When I was in Hospital wid a gouty leg—the sort of leg, ye know, that runs in families—the Captain looked afther me, and aftherwards tuk me for his servant. A fine young fellow he is too, and I'd not not like any mischance to happen him."

" Well," I said, " Is that all ? "

" It is not all, sor. Asking your pardon, you've a young lady here which is not suitable."

" Perhaps you will explain yourself."

" I will, sor. Ye see, the Captain's a Presbyter, like myself ; and the young lady being a Catholic, no good can come of it, and I'd take it kindly if ye'd forbid the banns."

" This is nonsense, Corporal McNeil."

"It is not nonsense, sor, for the Captain's not himself at all since he met the young lady ; and strange priests and suchlike keep calling at his quarters, which I take to be against the spirit of the Queen's regulations. But maybe ye know more about it than I do meself."

His keen, stern eye, that seemed to have a search-warrant in it, never left my face.

"What do you know about it, then?" I said.

"Just this—that the Captain's under close arrest, and there's threason in ut."

I think my utter, blank amazement restored me to the Corporal's good graces. He relaxed his Gorgon stare, and said, "If ye're the Captain's friend, ye'll maybe thrack down this divilment."

"You astound me, Corporal. But what is it all about—and how does the Captain endure suspicion?"

"It's threason that's about," replied McNeil, the square-set soldier. "As for the Captain, if ye'd been in battle as often as me, ye'd know there's two sets of men that fears nothing One is the downright infidel, that don't believe in this life nor the next; and the other is the Captain's sort, that thinks earth is just the recruitin' ground for Heaven. It's only the likes of him, and likes of the graceless reprobate, that can face death unflinching. A queer thing that is; but it's a thrue one."

An old friend of mine, formerly a surgeon in London practice, but who was now on the staff of the St. John's Ambulance, had dropt in upon me unexpectedly. At my request he visited Winifred, who was in a high fever; and he returned from the invalid's chamber just as McNeil was expounding his paradox. Tapping me on the shoulder, he said—"A carriage accident, you told me—*your niece is dying from a gunshot wound.* She is asking for some Captain—Fitz-William, I think—her cousin."

The room seemed to swim around me as the doctor spoke.

What happened during the next few moments I cannot say; but when recollection returned, I found myself with the doctor beside the bedside of the dying girl.

I implored, entreated, even commanded her to give me at least some clue to this strange tragedy; but to all my appeals she had only one reply.

"Oh, I cannot, I cannot—*he* has forbidden me, and the reverend father has forbidden me. I dare not break my vow."

"I will release you!" said the stern voice of O'Regan.

Dark, relentless, and forbidding he looked; and beside him stood his priestly familiar.

"This is no place for you, O'Regan" I said, with all the resolution I could assume.

"No; I am leaving you," he answered with a mocking laugh—"And I only regret that I cannot take the lady with me, more especially since she is my wife."

"Your wife, you traitor!" I exclaimed.

"Certainly, married a week ago—ask the *padre* there."

"O'Regan, I have a right to know"—

"Right! you have no rights, you chattering popinjay, and never will have now. But as a matter of courtesy—for you have been hospitable; yes, you have been hospitable, and pliable too, which is more to the purpose—I will keep you no longer in the dark. You have been pleased to call me traitor, and that I may be, but only from your point of view. If I were inclined to recriminate, I could show that it is you and

men like you who have betrayed your country. I have been
faithful to mine by being a deadly and—well, you would
call it unscrupulous—enemy to yours. But there is no need
to wear the mask now, and I will discard it."

"O'Regan, if you do not explain this, remember I can
compel you. I am a magistrate."

"A magistrate— so is the tinker at the street corner. We
are democratic now. But I will not keep you on tenter-
hooks. I have been playing a high game ; I have won, and
I can afford to be generous. It was essential for my
purposes to obtain the plan of a certain fortification, and
the only method I found practicable was through the medium
of your niece, whose cousin had access to them. And as the
young lady at first seemed obdurate, the reverend father here
helped to plead my suit."

The priest seemed about to remonstrate ; but O'Regan
stopped him.

"There is another dupe to be disillusioned"—he said
scornfully. "Reverend father, do you suppose we of the
new Socialist dispensation give credit to your auld wives'
tales ? Do you imagine we have used your ban, and book,
and bell, for any but our own purposes ? You have degraded
your holy office in the sight of the whole world, and the
fruit is rotten in your grasp. It is not the priest who will
be paramount in our new Republic."

"O'Regan," I said, "How can you talk thus by a death-
bed ?"

He started slightly, and I thought there was a touch of
anguish in his tone, as he said: "It is not fatal—it cannot
be. I know it is dangerous, but she shall not die."

Then, speaking wildly and rapidly, and as it seemed to
me like one *fey*—as the Scots term it—he told us how the
unhappy girl had been induced to aid him in his plot for
obtaining plans of the submarine defences of Landguard, and
how, as she was escaping incognita, the sentry fired into the
darkness with too true an aim.

Dazed and fainting, she contrived to reach the carriage
O'Regan had in readiness; and so eager was the plotter for
his spoil, that he at first failed to realise at what cost it
had been obtained. And now Winnie, beautiful, high-
spirited and accomplished, but—true type of the daughters of
Erin—changeful in her mood as the bosom of a mountain
lake, was dying, the victim of an ignoble adventurer.

"It is unfortunate; but the end justifies the means—eh,
holy father?" said O'Regan, bitterly.

"Oh, why could you not leave us unharmed?" murmured
Winnie—her thoughts turning to the true lover of her youth
—"we were happy until you came between us!"

"I will atone—I will atone!" exclaimed O'Regan, as
Winnie's white fingers fretted restlessly with the coverlet.
"When we have won you back to health you shall be the
first lady of the Irish-American Empire."

He bid her farewell, and was hastening away. But in

the vestibule I stopped him, my voice trembling with an emotion he did not fully comprehend.

"Time presses," he said impatiently. "You shall find me not ungrateful when we come to divide the spoil."

Now I had been blind, weak and wavering, misled by that Fetish I have named; but I was still an Englishman. And my anger being just then too vast for words, only one course occurred to me. I struck the traitor full in the face, and cried "I will denounce you, though I die for it!"

As I reeled to the wall under O'Regan's heavy hand, there stepped forward the Corporal I had left in the library.

From a hip pocket O'Regan snatched out a revolver, and covered him with it. He fired as the undaunted soldier advanced; but, with a shout that had in it more of triumph than of pain, the Corporal flung himself on the stalwart conspirator, and the men locked in furious conflict. At length they fell, O'Regan undermost. There was a sudden gleam of steel, and with a deep gasp, the Corporal sank helpless to the ground.

The murderer ("excited politicians," they were called in Gladstonese) leapt across the shrubbery, and disappeared.

Fitz-William was honourably acquitted by the Court-martial, my own evidence and Winnie's depositions sufficing to clear him. It was his voice that cheered her to the end; his hand that ranged the wreaths of immortelles on her lonely grave; his calm, strong spirit that upheld all around him through days when men's hearts were failing them for fear.

And those were terrible days indeed—the whole empire convulsed, and the agony of invasion intensified by civil broils; the vague mutterings of a social tempest that threatened to overwhelm our homes. The northern counties rallied splendidly, but at best they could only hold the enemy at bay, for he was reinforced constantly by hordes of American-Irish, whilst Ireland was one huge arsenal of munitions of war. And in our big towns the distress was daily growing more acute and formidable. With the establishment of Home Rule there had been an enormous exodus of capital from Loyalist Ireland; whilst Labour, leaving its ruined towns and deserted shipyards, thronged the English market until wages all round sank to starvation rates. And from the first days of the Dublin Parliament everything that Irish ingenuity could devise was done to vex our commerce; whilst in our own Parliament the Milesian element, wielding the balance of power, effectually blocked the measures devised by far-seeing statesmen for the strengthening of our defences and the much-needed improvement of our army. When at length Russia— its love of freedom outraged by our threatening the re-conquest of Ireland—flung down the gage of battle, France joined hands with the Muscovite, and drove us out of Egypt. Consols fell that week to 56; and when our forces were overwhelmed in India, the financial panic was indescribable. A lower depth, however, was touched when the combined fleet of the invaders set sail, and the distress of those whose incomes depended on public securities was pitiable as that of the hapless artisan and labourer. Our import and export trade seemed destined to reach the vanishing point, for only the swiftest cruisers dare venture on the high seas, and the Colonies were loth to trust their goods beneath the discredited English flag—the flag so soon to be ruthlessly trampled under foot. With droves of aliens too—the scum of every Continental state—in our metropolis, what wonder that we suffered from treachery on every hand? The enemy's system of espionage was perfect, and our most secret counsels were divulged. But I am again wandering into the region of history that has been so ably traversed by Naoroji; let me return to the bare record of my own experience.

A BOLT FROM THE BLUE.

Our long agony had a swift ending. Within a fortnight after O'Regan's disappearance, the enemy's fleet returned.

In accordance with the Scheme of Defence, the territorial regiments drawn from the wide region included within the Eastern Military District were massed between Colchester—which was crammed with military stores—and the coast line of north-east Essex. I was serving as a private in one of the auxiliary corps, for our need was so urgent that every man who had at any time carried a rifle was called out.

One night, whilst I was on outpost duty on the road that leads to Mersea Island, there came to me amidst the wailing of the wind, a sound so weird and terrible that I hope never to hear its like again. It was indeed "As though men fought on earth below, and fiends in upper air." I heard it only for a moment, and it passed away with the gust; but it froze me with a sudden horror; so that when my guard was relieved I could not sleep. Next morning the wildest rumours shook the Camp, and as the messages of disaster gained coherence, we learned that the sea-defences we relied on had been passed. By some occult means the enemy had escaped our torpedoes—it was said the wires that should have vitalised them had been tampered with—and having disembarked troops at Harwich, the invaders had landed a Division at Brightlingsea, on the Colne estuary, and were moving on Colchester Camp. All that day our troops streamed away to the front, and once fertile meadows were scarred by innumerable hoof-prints and worn bare by the track of wheels.

On the coast between Yarmouth and the mouth of the Thames were reared some of the hardiest seamen in Britain; indeed the whole male population was a strange amphibious race, ploughing land and water alternately, and wearing sea-boots almost from the cradle to the grave. From these had been recruited a marine militia, whose petty officers were chiefly old men-o'-war's men.

On that morning of "alarms and excursions," one of these old salts, whom I had known at Harwich, shouted a cheery greeting as his armed steam-launch grated against the quay by the riverside, where our Volunteer battalion was encamped; and it was he who gave me the first reliable news from the front. The enemy, he said, held either side of Harwich Harbour, and from Mersea Island they commanded the estuary of the Colne.

White-haired and weather-beaten, yet still hale and active, he seemed eager for the fray. "It minds me of old days outside Sebastopol," he said. "But I never thought to see French and Rooshans shipmates. Most everything that comes acrost a sailor-man has occurred to me—hunger, cold, shipwreck, and battle; and now me and a fleet of other old 'shell-backs' is goin' to finish our voyage in the old fighting style. We had a sarvice at the meetin' house last night—for I signed articles with the Wesleyans these ten years since, when the Bishop chartered a parson as burnt blue flares—incense, he called it—and now we're just ready for anything."

Then, chuckling with the glee of one possessing exclusive information, the old sea-dog gave me some startling news. O'Regan, he said, was with part of the invaders' force on Mersea Island, "And," added this ancient strategist, mysteriously, "say nowt to nobody; but he's goin' to be got at. It's through him them torpedoes was blinded, remember." "Full steam ahead," said the skipper of Marine Militia, and he started down the river to reconnoitre.

"THE DEUCE WINS."

Next morning we heard with dismay that our army corps was falling back on Colchester. Long trains of wounded passed into the town, and it was whispered that our position had been turned, and that the resource was *reculer pour mieux sauter.* But our difficulty was with the Irish regiments in garrison. These were undoubtedly disaffected ; emissaries such as O'Regan had been constantly at work amongst them. They had been politically educated by the Nationalist news-papers, and were told that the invasion was designed to protect the lives and liberty of Irishmen. Yet, to their honour be it spoken, as a body they were faithful to their salt. Desertions indeed were frequent, and insubordination was chronic, but the memory of the splendid services they had rendered when fighting shoulder to shoulder with Englishmen in the old glorious days of the United Empire, restrained them from casting in their lot with a foreign foe. Neverthe-less it was not thought politic to despatch them to the front, and we thus, at a critical moment, were unaided by the wild valour of those splendid soldiery.

It was about mid-day when the brigade to which our battalion was attached received the order to advance. The

sun's rays were, for the time of year, intensely powerful, and
I remember how grateful the older soldiers seemed for the
shade afforded in a cool hollow, where the road dipped
between high banks crowned with yellow gorse, and where a
break in a grove of tall poplars overshadowing a reedy waste,
afforded glimpses of the broad and glittering estuary of the
Colne—that once reflected the clustering masts of many a
fleet of pleasure yachts.   I say advisedly that the old soldiers
felt the heat ; but I know that most of us who had never
been under fire were in a cold shiver of apprehension.   This,
I learnt afterwards, is the usual experience of young soldiers,
and implies no dishonour to their manhood.   But inwardly
I seemed not nearly so heroic as I used to feel upon
parade.

Half a mile in front, our cavalry were moving into action
over a bluff and irregular country, shelving upwards in
pasture and arable, and intersected with faint green hedgerows.
Our guns were drawn up on the left flank, two squadrons
of Lancers screening them.   The red-coated Norfolk Volunteers, with the old "Two Fours" (44th), the "Pompadours"
(56th West Essex), the remnant of the "Marlborough's Own,"
and the slight active soldiers of the Bedford regiment, formed
our centre, whilst on our right were extended the trim grey-
clad battalions of the 1st and 2nd Herts. Volunteers and the
darker uniforms of the 2nd Essex.   Three strong Militia and
Volunteer regiments from Suffolk marched sturdily on our left.

At 3 p.m. the invaders' artillery opened from a rising

knoll that dominated the battle field. A sharp cavalry
skirmish resulted in the retreat of the Cossack squadrons, and
on all sides riderless horses galloped out of the battle. Our
infantry now swarmed into action, forming hastily into
extended order. A swift fusillade was exchanged, and flinch-
ing under the musketry and the big guns of the defending
army, the invaders sullenly fell back. Then in three thin,
well-ordered lines, moving like threads of scarlet across the
dull, amber-coloured surface of the sun-burnt plain, our centre
battalions advanced at the double, rolling back in a surging
wave the invaders' infantry. A loud cheer arose from our
reserves; but suddenly there was a new development. A
cloud of the enemy's light horsemen, hovering on the left
edge of the battle, galloped across the scrub in rear of their
own fighting line. Concealed and sheltered by a clump of
woodland, they reached the western limit of the field, just
beyond the right flank of their own infantry. Then they
wheeled left, and with wild yells charged at the film of scarlet.
But our line was resolute and ready. Through a rift in the
array of battle their keen eyes had caught the glint of
sabres as the cavalry flashed across that space behind the
wood. Quick as thought they formed rallying squares, and
poured into the invaders' cavalry a volley that emptied many
a saddle. One square that bore the brunt of the charge was
overwhelmed and sacrificed, but save for this disaster, the
bristling groups of redcoats held their own, and our artillery
opened point-blank upon the devoted troopers as they rode

back from their ill-starred charge. The defenders, with a victorious shout, advanced by companies in sharp and sudden rushes, but from their lofty eyrie the invaders' guns dropped shot and shell thickly in our ranks, and from behind an abattis of felled oak trees their sheltered riflemen poured in a withering fire. Whilst all this was happening, the 2nd Essex and the two Hertfordshire battalions had disappeared from the right of our fighting line. Led by officers of proved tactical skill, they effected a clever turning movement, and when the conflict was at its fiercest, and our centre, torn by shell and decimated by rifle fire, was falling back doggedly, the grey and dark green battalions suddenly struck the foe in flank, and drove them in full retreat upon their reserves. Cheering lustily, the Marlboroughs, Suffolks, and the old "Two Fours" then stormed the enemy's trenches on the hill, and there was wild work with the bayonet. If at this critical moment our supports had come promptly forward, the day must have been ours ; as it unhappily chanced they were formed by young soldiers recruited from the residuum of our big towns, and as the bursting shell fell amongst them, and the fierce thud of the bullet thinned their ranks, they wavered, broke, and melted from the field.

At sunset we still held our own positions ; but the attack upon the enemy's entrenchments had failed, and the town was filled with wounded. In the dusk of evening our men, labouring hard with pick and spade, threw up hasty entrenchments, protected by a fosse and by wire entanglements.

Fitz-William—through heavy casualties he was now the senior officer of · Royal Engineers whose services were available—proved himself the Vauban of our defence. His skill was marvellous ; his perfect fearlessness inspirited the troops, and aided by the good offices of one Father Kintore, Chaplain to the Forces, he charmed back to loyalty one of the renowned Irish regiments, whose fealty had been trembling in the balance.

This Father Kintore, by the way, was the very antithesis of the Jesuit with whom O'Regan had been involved. Young and ardent, his generous heart responding to the loftiest dictates of religion, and the truest impulses of patriotism, he was an ecclesiastic of the type we still meet, though at distant intervals, in every Christian Church, and who—whether English rector, Romish cardinal, or Wesleyan pastor -looks beyond the narrow pale of dogma, and tries to leave the world better than he found it. I saw little of him, but that little explained the reason of the friendship existing between the Orange Captain and this exceptional priest.

For two days we remained in our entrenchments, exchanging a desultory fire with the enemy's outposts. On the evening of the second day a sudden tumult broke out on the left of our line, and I saw an excited group of soldiery advancing, waving their helmets, and cheering wildly. In the centre of the ·mob marched a half-troop of Lancers, and it was evident that prisoners were being brought in.

"The Spy, the Spy !" was the refrain of that soldiers'

chorus ; and then I knew that the old "shellback" had kept
his word. The proudest man in the Queen's service that day
was that ancient mariner, as he explained how he had surprised and captured O'Regan in his tent on Mersea Island.
"We dropped down on 'em in the dark," he said. "And
when he saw the Corporal that he thought was under the
turf, he swooned right off, and we lumped him into the
launch, and steamed away."

And in effect, Corporal McNeil, pale but resolute, was
standing by the old sailor's side, having proved tougher than
anyone not acquainted with North of Ireland men could have
imagined.

That night the enemy's fire increased, but our men were
hardening to it, and in the earthwork where O'Regan awaited
the gallows, his captors sat with their knees under a rough
plank, playing cards. At length one of the party left for
picquet duty, and the prisoner, either feigning or actually
feeling a keen interest in the game, asked to be allowed a
hand in it. With rough jests the guard assented, and
loosening the cords on O'Regan's legs—the ligatures had
been made taut by the simple process of twisting them
with a cleaning-rod, tourniquet-fashion—they released his
arms. He played to the admiration of his captors,
and in the third game, starting to his feet, he flung an ace
on the board, and exclaimed "The Deuce wins!" At that
moment he fell forward—dead. A shell, hissing as it left
the dark belt of firs that screened the enemy's central

battery, had burst just in front of the earthwork; a splinter struck the prisoner's head the instant he raised it above the parapet.

"He was in luck to-night—but now we must play dummy," remarked one of the party.

They laid the body outside the earthwork, and went on with the game.

What happened after our brush with the enemy before Colchester all the world knows. Avoiding the garrison town, which had been strongly fortified, the enemy suddenly marched across country from Mersea Island to Witham, where they seized the railway station, and despatched huge bodies of troops by rail to Chelmsford. Other forces sailing in light draught vessels up the Blackwater were landed at Maldon. The little town, admirably posted for defence, resisted stubbornly, but was taken by assault after some furious street fighting, in which the Gardner guns of the Essex Volunteers were smartly-handled, and proved very effective. The enemy, however, exasperated by their losses, sacked and burnt the town, committing terrible excesses. Establishing a base at Chelmsford, they then detached two vast columns to march on London, *viâ* Chipping Ongar and Brentwood. The Brentwood column, failing to capture Warley by a *coup de main*, left a force there to hold the garrison in check, and continued their march on London, which was also threatened by a naval force hovering at the mouth of the Thames. In ferocity and in pitiless destruction of human life, the battles fought on the north-east of London surpassed the most ghastly records of the century. Where War, as Wellington and Moltke understood it, had slain thousands, Science—our vaunted Science—destroyed millions.

When I think of those terrible days, and of the friends and kinsmen I lost—

> " A thousand fantasies
> Begin to throng into my memory,
> Of calling shapes and beckoning shadows dire ;
> And airy tongues, that syllable men's names
> On sands, and shores, and desert wildernesses."

And the ruin of an empire, the death of millions, the destruction of inestimable treasure, resulted from the unchecked vanity of an octogenarian orator who preferred to wreck his country rather than own himself mistaken.

To our highly civilised, and therefore enervated community, the shock of accomplished invasion was the more terrible, because that invasion had long been declared impossible. And our social troubles contributed to our downfall. We were paralysed by internal dissensions. The discontent stirred up in our big towns by professional politicians, was increased by the glut in the urban labour market resulting from the failure of agriculture. The adze and the mill were idle because the plough lay rusting in the furrow ; lands once happy and fertile were abandoned to the coney and the fox ; whilst the forlorn husbandman jostled the artisan in a fierce struggle for bare existence.

And now I have said my say. Fitz-William, who won distinction in the war, now holds a high military command in the League of the Southern Cross ; whilst I, once a wealthy English manufacturer, have nothing I can call my own. But though Great Britain met the fate of Carthage and of Rome, no military combination could subjugate the great Anglo-Saxon race. "The Great Betrayal" resulted merely in a transference of power—not indeed from west to east, but from England to the great Australian Continent.

> "So sinks the day-star in the ocean-bed,
> And yet anon repairs his drooping head,
> And tricks his beams, and with new-spangled ore
> Flames in the forehead of the morning sky."

www.ingramcontent.com/pod-product-compliance
Lightning Source LLC
Chambersburg PA
CBHW021642270326
41931CB00008B/1127